Toby and Trish
and the Amazing Book of
John

Text copyright © Margaret Spivey 2000
Illustrations copyright © Tom Hewitt 2000
The author asserts the moral right to be identified as the
author of this work.
Published by **The Bible Reading Fellowship**
Peter's Way, Sandy Lane West
Oxford OX4 5HG
ISBN 1 84101 121 5
First edition 2000
10 9 8 7 6 5 4 3 2 1 0
Acknowledgments
Scripture quotations are taken from the Good News Bible
published by The Bible Societies/HarperCollins Publishers
Ltd UK © American Bible Society, 1966, 1971, 1976, 1992.
A catalogue record for this book is available from the
British Library.
Printed and bound in Great Britain by Caledonian Book
Manufacturing International, Glasgow.

Toby and Trish
(and Boomerang!)
and the Amazing Book of

John

Feed this dog

by Margaret Spivey

Illustrated by Tom Hewitt

Welcome to the Amazing Book of John!

The great detective story

No one is absolutely sure who wrote this book. But we can be fairly certain that John, son of Zebedee, brother of James and friend of Jesus, had a lot to do with it. John was always close to Jesus. He watched. He listened carefully. He talked to witnesses. For many years he examined the evidence. And here it is at last—the book that tells us:

- Who Jesus is
- Where he came from
- Why he came
- What he meant by what he said

Together with Toby and Trish, let's be detectives and find out what all this has to do with us!

Light!
John 1:1-9

The light shines in the darkness, and the darkness has never put it out. (Verse 5)

The north coast of Scotland is fringed with dangerous rocks. Many ships have sailed too close on dark, stormy nights. They were smashed on the rocks, and hundreds of sailors perished. But two hundred years ago the Stevenson family started building lighthouses—they were called 'The Lighthouse Stevensons'. Because of these warning lights, thousands of lives were saved. (A member of the family, Robert Louis Stevenson, describes one of the lighthouses in his great adventure story, *Kidnapped!*)

When God made the universe, he first made—light. And now here is John opening his book by introducing another John—John the Baptist, who came with this message: Jesus is the light of the world. However dark things seem to be, his light is always shining.

Dear Jesus, thank you that we need never be afraid of the dark, because you are always there. Amen

5

The first word a baby says is 'Daddy'

God's living word
John 1:10-14

That's because Mummy teaches it...

The Word became a human being and, full of grace and truth, lived among us. We saw his glory, the glory which he received as the Father's only Son. (Verse 14)

I need a new dictionary. I can't find 'video' or 'e-mail' in my old one, because it's out of date. Words are important. There are about a quarter of a million of them—and that's just in English! Words can be healing—words like 'thank you', 'sorry' and 'I love you' can bring peace. They can be dangerous—they can bring unhappiness and start wars.

Jesus was with God from the very beginning. And now he is God's way of showing us what God is like. He is God's 'word'. Because of Jesus, we can know what God is like and hear his words.

Father God, thank you for sending your Son Jesus to show how much you love us. Amen

Rules and regulations
John 1:15-18

God gave the Law through Moses, but grace and truth came through Jesus Christ. (Verse 17)

'Keep off the grass.' 'Fasten your seat belt.' 'No running in the corridors.'

Everywhere we go, there are notices telling us how to behave. We need rules. The government makes laws to protect us and keep us safe. If we all did exactly as we wanted, we would soon run into trouble.

Long before Jesus lived on earth, God gave Moses a set of rules. We call them the Ten Commandments. When we stick to them, the world is a happier place. People had known this for hundreds of years. But now John the Baptist brings some amazing news about Jesus. God has given us rules, but he's also given us his Son, Jesus, to show the rule of love and truth.

Who are you?
John 1:19-28

The Jewish authorities in Jerusalem sent some priests and Levites to John, to ask him, 'Who are you?' (Verse 19)

At Anthony's birthday party, there was a boy I hadn't met before. I said, 'Hello, I'm Mrs Spivey.' He looked blank, so I added 'Margaret Spivey'. He said, 'Oh, hello,' and walked away. I saw him whisper to Anthony, 'Who's that lady?' and Anthony replied, 'Oh, that's my mum.' He looked so relieved—at last he knew who I was!

Those people asked John who he was three times. But John didn't want to talk about himself. He wanted to talk about Jesus. Unfastening sandals was such an awful job that a servant could refuse to do it. Only a slave couldn't refuse. John didn't think he was good enough even to be Jesus' slave.

Thank you, Jesus, that I can be sure of who I am in your sight. Amen

Can you prove it?
John 1:29-34

And John gave this testimony: 'I saw the Spirit come down like a dove from heaven and stay on him.' (Verse 32)

A birth certificate is a small piece of paper but it's important because it proves that we are who we say we are. Our name, date and place of birth—they're all there. We must show it when we need a passport. We need it when we want to get married. It's no good just saying, 'I'm Felicity Bloggs'—even if you are. You have to prove it.

God didn't send a piece of paper fluttering out of the sky. But he did send a very special bird. In Jesus' day, the dove was protected and considered very holy. John knew that this was Jesus' 'birth certifcate'. It proved he was God's Son.

John 1:1-34
Things to do

Cotton through here ↓ *

Dove story

Trace the shape of the dove on to thin card and cut it out. Slip a length of cotton through the hole at the top and tie it to make a loop.

Write the words, 'He is the Son of God' on the dove and hang it in your bedroom to remind you of the beginning of John's Gospel.

Toby + Trish Dove joint

I made it at school. It's called a dove-tail joint!

Is that why it keeps flying apart?

We try to talk and swap jokes in class, but we get shushed

Getting to know you
John 1:35-42

'Come and see,' he answered. (It was then about four o'clock in the afternoon.) So they went with him and saw where he lived, and spent the rest of that day with him. (Verse 39)

The Kids' Klub meet every Friday. They play games and have fun. But after an hour it's time to go home. There's never time to get to know one another really well. But when they go on an outing, or camping, that's different. Then there's time to talk and swap jokes and ideas.

Imagine being able to do that with Jesus—to see where he lived, to relax and have a meal with him!

The great news is that we needn't say 'Hello' and 'Goodbye' to Jesus only once a week. If we spend time getting to know him, we'll be able to say, like Andrew, 'We have found the Messiah'—the person promised by God long ago.

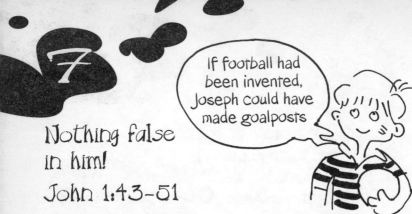

If football had been invented, Joseph could have made goalposts

Nothing false in him!
John 1:43-51

'Can anything good come from Nazareth?'
Nathanael asked. 'Come and see,' answered
Philip. (Verse 46)

Jesus had invited Philip to go to Galilee with him! Philip was bursting to tell someone about Jesus, so he told Nathanael.

Nathanael's home town, Cana, was only 18 kilometres from Nazareth. Jesus had friends there. They were two small towns in Galilee. If football had been invented then, there might have been matches Cana v Nazareth. So Nathanael jeered, 'Nazareth? Rubbish!'

We always think our town's best, and of course we support our team. But we must take care. Rivalry can turn to hatred.

Nathanael had nothing to worry about. Jesus knew he was a good man. And Nathanael recognized his Lord and King.

Dear Jesus, I pray that you'll always
be able to say that there's nothing
false in me. Amen

No half measures
John 2:1-10

When the wine had given out, Jesus' mother said to him, 'They have no wine left.' (Verse 3)

Horror! Disaster! A wedding could go on for two weeks—and they'd run out of wine! The family would be disgraced. But Jesus was their friend. So he went into action—with his first miracle.

When people try a new job, they usually start with something small. If you'd never used an oven before, you might make a few biscuits. You wouldn't make a fancy wedding cake, would you? But Jesus was different. If you really want to know what he did, it went like this:

Six water jars full to the brim, each holding about one hundred litres. A litre equals about six glasses of wine. Now work it out with a calculator: 6 x 100 x 6. That's how many glasses of wine there were! (The answer is at the bottom of the page.) Don't worry, it wouldn't have been strong enough to get everyone horribly drunk.

So when we ask Jesus for something, we'd better watch out!

Jesus protests
John 2:11-17

So he made a whip from cords and drove all the animals out of the Temple, both the sheep and the cattle; he overturned the tables of the money-changers and scattered their coins. (Verse 15)

The car knocked Jamie flying and smashed his arm. It was the third accident on that crossing in six months. Jamie's mother was angry. But she prayed, and God showed her what to do. She organized a parents' protest. They painted banners and got permission from the police to march to the town hall. It worked: the town council paid for a safe crossing-place.

Jesus was very angry. Inside the temple, people were being cheated. And how could anyone pray with all that noise—coins clattering and animals bleating? Yes, Jesus made a whip, but only to drive the animals out.

Sometimes it's right to feel angry. But we should always ask God what to do about it.

I can worship God just as well on my bike

Yes, but DO YOU?

The real temple
John 2:18-25

Jesus answered, 'Tear down this Temple, and in three days I will build it again.' (Verse 19)

Jesus was angry when people misused the temple. But the building itself wasn't important. There had been a wooden temple long before, and that had burnt down. Then a stone one had been destroyed. And Jesus knew that this one would be destroyed, too.

We know something that those people didn't know. Jesus would die and God would raise him to life again after three days. Yes, Jesus meant the temple of his body. The temple in Jerusalem was destroyed later, but we still have Jesus.

It's how we worship God that matters, not where. And God's Holy Spirit will always show us the way.

Lord Jesus, please help me to worship God in a way that pleases you. Amen

Things to do

Mary and Jesus
are invited
to a wedding
at Cana.

Wedding invitation

This is one of the happiest stories in the whole book. Imagine you are enjoying a lovely party. You can hear the bees buzzing in the summer garden. Make an invitation and decorate it with the things you see and hear.

Toby + Trish — At the wedding

I love dressing up! It's lovely being a bridesmaid. I can't wait for it to start!

I can't wait for it to finish!

Trish used to be so lovable!

A fresh start
John 3:1-11

Jesus answered, 'I am telling you the truth: no one can see the Kingdom of God without being born again.' (Verse 3)

Have you ever played a video in reverse? It's hilarious, with everything running and jumping backwards. It's fun, but we know it's only a trick.

Nicodemus was right. In real life we can't shrink back to baby size, with no teeth or hair. But Jesus was right, too. Look at a new baby and see for yourself. Babies don't tell fibs, argue, or lose their tempers. They get hungry, but never greedy. The Kingdom of God is made up of people like that—thanking, trusting and loving.

Jesus helps us to make a fresh start—trusting God for all we need, thanking him, and loving him.

Dear Lord, thank you that with your help I can make a fresh start every day. Amen

So much love
John 3:12–21

For God loved the world so much that he gave his only Son, so that everyone who believes in him may not die but have eternal life. (Verse 16)

This is my favourite verse of all time

In Thailand there's a graveyard for soldiers who died in World War Two. Thousands of prisoners were ill-treated and starved. Young men from Britain, Australia, New Zealand and other places died far away from home. They died fighting to keep the world safe for you and me. They gave their lives. But if you asked their parents, 'Will you give your only son?' how many would say 'Yes'? Not many. Sons and daughters are very precious.

God loved his Son, but he loves us too. 'The world' doesn't just mean planet Earth—it means you and me. And amazingly, when we love Jesus, we become God's children, too.

Even the back legs of the horse have got to dance!

Gifts from God
John 3:22-30

John answered, 'No one can have anything unless God gives it to him.' (Verse 27)

Gloria was beautiful. She could sing and dance. I was jealous. Why hadn't God made me like Gloria? But he'd given me different gifts.

It was a pantomime that made me understand. In the panto were people of all ages, with every gift under the sun. Danny said, 'I'm no good at anything: I'll be the back legs of the horse.' Suddenly he discovered his gift—clowning! And me? Well, God had given me a gift for sewing, and I made the costumes. It was a brilliant panto!

John the Baptist wasn't jealous of Jesus. He knew God had given him a special job. He was happy just to see Jesus taking first place.

Dear God, please show me how to use the special gifts you've given me, for you. Amen

Love—powerful stuff
John 3:31-36

The Father loves his Son, and has put everything in his power. (Verse 35)

I have a son called Anthony. He's a fine young man, and we love him. He uses everything we have at home—the TV, the fridge, the washing-machine. We let him drive our car. We don't just love him: we trust him. It's good to feel the way we do. Even so, there are limits. We can only give him what we have.

But John is speaking about God's Son. And God gave his Son something we can never give ours—the power to give you and me eternal life! Yes, God gave Jesus everything: all his Spirit, and all his power. God says, 'It's all yours, Son.' If God trusts Jesus, so can we.

Jesus takes a short cut
John 4:1-9

So when Jesus heard what was being said, he left Judea and went back to Galilee; on his way there he had to go through Samaria. (Verses 3 and 4)

There's a short cut from my house to the postbox. But it's a dark, narrow path, so I usually go the long way round.

You could walk from Judea to Galilee through Samaria in three days. If you walked round Samaria, it took six days. But, for the Jews, Samaria was enemy territory. Jesus' friends must have been nervous. They were hungry, too.

I've just found a short cut to the sweet shop

Sometimes God allows us into strange places. A new house, school, church or club can be scary. We're not sure we'll be welcome. People might tease us because we're different. But it's all part of the adventure of growing up. And if God lets us go there, he'll be there with us.

John 3:1—4:9
Things to do

A picture of the wind

Jesus uses a picture of the wind to describe the Holy Spirit. Draw some ways that we see the wind. Here are some to start you off.

Toby + Trish — Bitter blow

Jesus and the Samaritan woman
John 4:1Ø–15

'Whoever drinks the water that I will give him will never be thirsty again.' (Verse 14a)

Our tap water is good, but if I want spring water I have to buy a bottle at the supermarket. The Samaritan woman had neither tap nor supermarket! For her, collecting water was hard work. She used a leather bucket on a cord to fill a big clay pot. She had to carry the pot home on her shoulder. And water from the well was never as good as sparkling spring water.

Jesus offered her something amazing: spring water inside her that is always fresh, never runs out, and gives eternal life! She knew the promise that God had made long before: when the Messiah came, 'the dry land would be filled with springs'. She begged Jesus for that water. But first she had to discover who he was!

17

Guess what I've just heard!

I am he
John 4:16-26

The woman said to him, 'I know that the Messiah will come, and when he comes, he will tell us everything.' Jesus answered, 'I am he, I who am talking with you.' (Verses 25 and 26)

Here was Jesus talking to a woman, and a Samaritan. No one else would have done such a thing! But Jesus had three more amazing things to tell this woman. First, he knew she had been married five times, and wasn't married now. Next he told her that where we worship God isn't important. It's how that matters, and God's Holy Spirit helps us to worship him as we should.

Lastly, Jesus told her the most amazing news of all—that he was the Messiah, the one promised by God long ago. No wonder she couldn't wait to tell everyone.

 *Dear Jesus, thank you for keeping your promise, and telling us so much. Amen*

Real food
John 4:27-35

'My food,' Jesus said to them, 'is to obey the will of the one who sent me and to finish the work he gave me to do.' (Verse 34)

It's so annoying. You're in the middle of something really important and somebody calls, 'Dinner's ready!' You can't wait to finish what you're doing. Until you have, you can't even think about food.

The disciples thought Jesus must be hungry. But his mind was on other things. In that dry land there weren't many places where corn would grow. Sychar was in one of those areas. Perhaps Jesus could see waving corn. Perhaps he could see people hurrying from the town to see him.

Jesus saw those things and thought of a harvest— of people. People needed to be gathered in, safe with him for ever. That was his work—and the 'food' he needed.

GRUB UP!

19

Potatoes are down there somewhere

Harvest time
John 4:36-42

'The saying is true, "One sows, another reaps."' (Verse 37)

There's an apple tree in our garden. Someone planted it long before we moved here. They pruned it, fed it and cared for it. Now all we have to do is to pick the fruit. There's enough to share with our neighbours. I hate to waste those apples! I hope that long after I've gone people will enjoy the grapes from the vine we've planted.

It's the same with God's harvest of people. Even if we don't talk about Jesus, a kind act or word may start people thinking about him. We'll have sown a seed. If it grows, someone will harvest it later. We may never know. And one day Jesus may ask us to do some reaping.

Dear Lord, help me to be ready to sow or reap—whichever you choose. Amen

Remote control
John 4:43-54

Jesus said to him, 'Go, your son will live!' (Verse 50)

Could you deliver two pizzas, please?

My friend Ann phoned from Scotland. 'I have to go to hospital tomorrow for an operation!' Whatever could I do? I live miles away. I phoned a flower nursery in Guernsey. The next day, a big bunch of freesias arrived at Ann's hospital, hundreds of miles away.

Today we can make things happen at the press of a button. But it wasn't so easy in those days. Why would an important man walk twenty miles to ask a carpenter for help? His son was dying. He loved him very much. And he believed what he'd heard about Jesus. He believed Jesus could heal his son.

That man had already pressed the 'faith' button. All Jesus had to do was to say the word, and the boy lived. His father's faith, and Jesus' word, had saved him.

John 4:10-54
Things to do

The well at Sychar

The well would have been a shady, white building with lots of steps to sit on, out of the heat. Colour this picture of Jesus and the woman chatting on the steps of the well.

Toby + Trish Well...

I'd much rather get water from a well!

Why?

Whoever heard of a wishing-tap?

I couldn't have done my homework last night, because I knew I wasn't going to be well today!

I don't feel well

John 5:1-9a

Jesus saw him lying there, and he knew that the man had been ill for such a long time; so he asked him, 'Do you want to get well?' (Verse 6)

When my granny was getting old, my mother used to visit her every day. One day, Mum told Granny, 'Next Tuesday I'm going to Windermere for the day. I'm really looking forward to it. I've asked Mrs Smith to pop in.'

But Granny didn't like Mrs Smith. When Mum went round on Monday, Granny didn't feel well. The doctor said she must stay in bed. So Mum missed her day out. Granny was soon well again.

Do you know people like that? They don't want to do something, so they get stomach-ache.

Someone had looked after the man who had been ill for thirty-eight years. Did he really want to get well? It was a good question. We can fool others, but we can't fool Jesus.

A warning
John 5:9b–15

Afterwards, Jesus found him in the Temple and said, 'Listen, you are well now; so stop sinning or something worse may happen to you.' (Verse 14)

I'd love to know what the man was doing, wouldn't you? Perhaps he was showing off. Whatever it was, Jesus wasn't pleased.

It's easy to promise 'I'll be good' whenever we wriggle out of trouble. We really mean it. Then somehow we forget. Being forgiven is great, but it should be a fresh start, not an excuse to start bad habits again.

Jesus went looking for that man. He went to warn him. That's the lovely thing about Jesus. He doesn't just help, then forget about us. He cares what happens next.

Dear Jesus, I don't want to let you down. Thanks for warning me when things are going wrong in my life. Amen

His Father's business
John 5:16-23

'For the Father loves the Son and shows him all that he himself is doing. He will show him even greater things to do than this, and you will all be amazed.' (Verse 20)

Corrie ten Boom's father was a watchmaker in Holland. She helped in his shop. He taught her to mend watches. Later she went to training school, and became the first woman watchmaker in Holland. But it was delicate work, and Corrie often asked the Lord to lay his hand on hers as she worked. And she and her father prayed together. Mr ten Boom said it was a joy to teach his own daughter.

Her heavenly Father had other plans for Corrie ten Boom, but she never forgot the patience she learned from her earthly father, or the joy they had together.

Heavenly Father, thank you for teaching me so willingly. Amen

24

Not guilty
John 5:24-30

'I am telling you the truth: those who hear my words and believe in him who sent me have eternal life. They will not be judged, but have already passed from death to life.' (Verse 24)

People are scared about lots of things—about things they've done wrong in the past, about what they're like now, about death, about being judged. If you're ever scared, just look at what Jesus says here!

This verse has only thirty-four words, so perhaps you could memorize it. If not, remember these three things:

- If you tell Jesus you're really sorry for bad things you've done, he doesn't just forgive—he forgets. They're cancelled.
- He doesn't care whether you're young or old, fat or thin—he loves you the way you are. So there's nothing to judge.
- If you listen to Jesus and believe him, you needn't be afraid. You'll live with him for ever—starting from now.

Isn't that worth remembering?

Don't take my word for it
John 5:31-40

'If I testify on my own behalf, what I say is not to be accepted as real proof.' (Verse 31)

Vicky saw the notice in the shop window, and stepped inside. 'I'd like the job of paper-girl, please.' The lady stared at her. 'Are you really fourteen? It's hard work, and I'd have to trust you to collect the money.' Vicky said 'Yes' to all those things.

The lady still wasn't sure. 'Ask your teacher or someone from church to write a testimonial for you. Then I'll think about it.' Vicky did as she was asked, and got the job.

Yes, we need proof that we can be trusted. But the person who gives that proof must be trustworthy, too. There's a saying, 'Actions speak louder than words.' The actions God had given Jesus to do were his testimonial.

John 5:1-40

Things to do

Visitors' book

When you stay in a hotel, or visit a church, you are invited to say what you thought about it in the visitors' book.

Imagine that someone stays at your house. What would they write in your visitors' book and why?

Toby + Trish   Visitors' book

I can never think what to put

EASY! Just write, 'What can I say...'

Apple pie! TERRIFIC!

SCRUMMY!

Who do you believe?

John 5:41-46

'You like to receive praise from one another, but you do not try to win praise from the one who alone is God; how, then, can you believe me?' (Verse 44)

When Joyce makes an apple pie, her family say, 'Thanks, Mum' and eat the lot. But when Joe says, 'Excellent!' she's delighted. You see, Joe's a pastry chef. He's checked that the pastry is light and crisp. He knows that the apples are moist and not too sweet. If Joe says it's good, Joyce knows it must be true.

These people in Jerusalem loved to argue. They argued about what Moses had said. They argued with John the Baptist. They argued with each other. They argued with Jesus. He was the expert on love, but they'd forgotten to love God.

If we love someone, we don't just argue. We want to understand them, and please them.

Just testing
John 6:1-7

Jesus looked round and saw that a large crowd was coming to him, so he asked Philip, 'Where can we buy enough food to feed all these people?'
(Verse 5)

Jesus was tired—until he saw five thousand people coming towards him. Then he forgot about himself. They had walked for miles, and they were hungry.

First Jesus asked Philip, and Philip wasn't much help! But at least he'd thought about it. He'd worked out how much it would cost. So Jesus didn't say, 'You've failed, you're no good.' He never does. He knows it takes time to see things his way. (You'll read more about Philip later.) And he's got lots of patience. If we don't get things right the first time, we can try again later.

Thank you, Jesus, that you keep 'just testing', and give us time to learn to do things your way. Amen

Jesus gives thanks
John 6:8-15

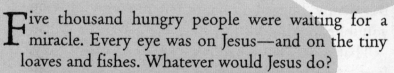

Jesus took the bread,
gave thanks to God,
and distributed it to
the people who
were sitting there.
He did the same
with the fish, and they
all had as much as they
wanted. (Verse 11)

Five thousand hungry people were waiting for a miracle. Every eye was on Jesus—and on the tiny loaves and fishes. Whatever would Jesus do?

Well, Jesus did what Jewish fathers did at home. Before he performed any miracle, he thanked God for those scraps of food. He said something like this: 'Blessed are you, O Lord our God, King of the Universe, who brings forth bread from the earth.'

Philip had said, 'It's hopeless.' But Jesus said, 'Thank you, God.'

By the way, after any feast the leftovers were collected in baskets and given to the servants as a 'thank you' to take home. There was one for each disciple. Coincidence?

I got lost on the sponsored walk, but they came and picked me up in a car

He's always there

John 6:16–21

Night came on, and Jesus still had not come to them. (Verse 17b)

Jenny took a wrong turning in a department store, and got horribly lost. Her mother searched high and low. She found Jenny at last, miserable and scared. But Jenny hugged her mother and said, 'I knew you'd be looking for me.'

That night, Jesus had gone off somewhere alone. It was late. His friends didn't expect to see him for a while. What a shock they had when he appeared, walking on the water! But it was full moon. Jesus could have been watching the boat from the hillside. And he knew about the strong winds and rough waves.

Jesus is the good friend who's always there when we need him.

Dear Jesus, we can't always see you, but we know you're always there. Thank you. Amen

No sell-by date
John 6:22–29

'Do not work for food that goes bad; instead, work for the food that lasts for eternal life.' (Verse 27a)

I love candyfloss, chocolate fudge and ice-cream, but I know what would happen if I ate nothing else. I'd get fat and sick, and all my teeth would rot and fall out!

The bread and fish were nourishing, but only for a few hours. Soon they would go stale. Next they'd begin to smell. Then they'd turn mouldy and slimy. It's true of food. But it can also be true of other things we enjoy—games, music, the clothes we wear. Even if they don't go bad, we can grow out of them. They can become boring, a waste of time and energy. But Jesus gives the food that's healthy and nourishing: there's no sell-by date on anything Jesus gives.

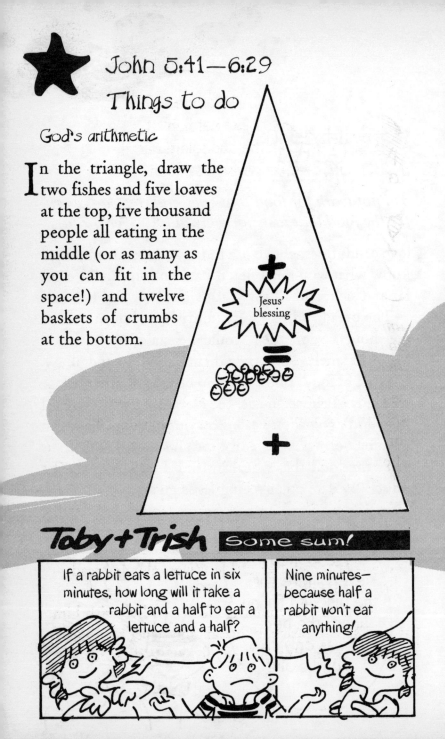

John 5:41—6:29
Things to do

God's arithmetic

In the triangle, draw the two fishes and five loaves at the top, five thousand people all eating in the middle (or as many as you can fit in the space!) and twelve baskets of crumbs at the bottom.

Jesus' blessing

Toby + Trish — Some sum!

If a rabbit eats a lettuce in six minutes, how long will it take a rabbit and a half to eat a lettuce and a half?

Nine minutes—because half a rabbit won't eat anything!

Great idea!
I just eat half of
the chocolate bar
every day, then
it will last
for ever!

The bread of life
John 6:30-40

'I am the bread of life,' Jesus told them. 'Those who come to me will never be hungry; those who believe in me will never be thirsty.' (Verse 35)

The telephone rings. A voice says, 'Congratulations, you've won a prize.' It sounds exciting, but you soon learn that there's a catch in it.

Long ago, when the Israelites were in the desert with Moses, God had sent 'manna' for them to eat. It was good, but only for one day. The second day it turned rotten and wormy. The Israelites soon got bored with it. Jesus remembered all this. But the people only remembered that it was miracle bread—and they wanted it.

Jesus offers everyone the chance to live with him for ever, to eat 'heavenly bread' and never be hungry or thirsty again. But did they listen? Well, some did.

32

That chocolate bar wasn't chocolatey enough. I had to eat it all!

Enjoy!
John 6:41-50

Jesus answered, 'Stop grumbling among yourselves.' (Verse 43)

During World War Two, Corrie ten Boom spent years in a Nazi concentration camp. Then she spent the rest of her life telling people about God's love.

One day, soon after the war, she was teaching the Bible to some foreign women. They listened stony-faced. To them, she was just an ignorant Dutch woman. They disagreed with everything she taught. The next day she took them a bar of Dutch chocolate and shared it with them. (It was soon after the war, and chocolate was very scarce.) They thanked her, ate the chocolate—and this time they smiled.

Corrie gently pointed out how happy they'd been with her gift. They hadn't asked where it was made, how much it cost, or how many calories there were in it! Why couldn't they enjoy God's word like that?

Life everlasting
John 6:
51-58

'I am the living bread that came down from heaven. If anyone eats this bread, he will live for ever.' (Verse 51a)

Emma's granny couldn't get to her birthday party. So she made a beautiful birthday cake. Although she wasn't rich, she bought the finest ingredients— cherries, almonds, eggs, butter and marzipan. She decorated it and posted it 'Special Delivery'. Emma shouted, 'It looks fantastic—but it's too good to eat!' and put it away carefully in her bedroom.

When Granny visited a few months later, Emma proudly showed her the cake. 'It's beautiful,' she said. 'I look at it every week.'

Granny was so sad. The cake had cost her a great deal. It would have been tasty and nourishing when she sent it. But now, beneath all the fancy icing, it wasn't fit to eat.

Thank you, Jesus, that the food you give is for eating, and lasts for ever. Amen

43

Switch on!
John 6:59-65

'What gives life is God's Spirit; human power is of no use at all. The words I have spoken to you bring God's life-giving Spirit.' (Verse 63)

I use a computer for writing. At the back of the handbook there's a problem page. It suggests things to do if the screen doesn't light up. The first suggestion is 'Make sure you're switched on.' The computer's very clever, but it won't work if I plug it into the gas cooker or the garden hose. It needs electricity. First I have to plug it in, then switch it on.

Jesus had tried to explain to these people at Capernaum. God had sent him to give them eternal life, but it only worked from the inside. He had brought them God's words and God's Spirit. But unless they plugged in and switched on, they would be powerless.

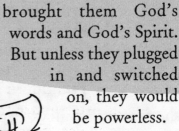

It is safe to switch me off

Go for it!
John 6:66-71

Simon Peter answered him, 'Lord, to whom should we go? You have the words that give eternal life.' (Verse 68)

Tony had been out of work for months. Then he was offered a job in a remote, dangerous part of Africa. Should he take it? Or should he stay where he was, unemployed but safe? Well, he took it. It was the most exciting time of his life.

The authorities were after Jesus. For those who followed him, life might be dangerous. They'd seen the miracles, but now the fun was over. Many turned away. They could smell danger.

Simon Peter understood, but for him there was only one choice. Now that he knew Jesus, life would never be the same again.

Lord Jesus, help me to be like Simon Peter— ready to follow you, no matter what. Amen

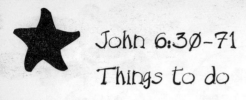

John 6:30-71
Things to do

Life without bread!

Here are some cartoons of people missing bread. Fill in what they are saying in the speech bubbles.

My brother doesn't believe I can boil an egg!

Jesus and his brothers
John 7:1-11

Not even his brothers believed in him. (Verse 5)

The Festival of Shelters was an exciting time. For seven days around the time of full moon, there was fun and rejoicing. The Jews called it simply 'The Festival'.

Jesus knew that the authorities would be looking for him when it started. It would be safer for him to go a few days later. He wasn't lying to his brothers about who he was, just being cautious.

His family had always known he was different. There was that time in Jerusalem when he was twelve. His parents had thought he was lost, but when they found him in the temple he asked them, 'Didn't you know that I had to be in my Father's house?'

How could his brothers understand? Later they did understand, and James became the leader of the church in Jerusalem. But that's another story.

37

Jesus at the Festival

John 7:12-20

'How does this man know so much when he has never had any training?' (Verse 15b)

Most of us have to take exams sooner or later. Even if we're brilliant at something—swimming, music, Japanese—it's no good just telling people. Sometimes we need a certificate to prove it.

Three quarters of the Bible had been written before Jesus was born. All Jewish boys read it. Jesus had read it, studied it—and understood. But he hadn't taken any exams. And he didn't show off. He didn't want glory for himself. He wanted it for God, his Father.

The great news is that God is our Father, too—our heavenly Father—and he has promised to teach us everything that he taught Jesus. Isn't that amazing?

*Dear Jesus, **thank you that we can know about God's love without being brilliant. Amen***

Loud and clear
John 7:21-29

'Stop judging by external standards, and judge by true standards.'
(Verse 24)

Jesus was getting fed up. He'd tried so hard to make people understand, to make them see what really mattered. But they weren't listening. Some liked his miracles—they were exciting. Others complained because he'd healed on the Sabbath—that was breaking the law. They weren't really listening to what he said. At last he spoke up and told them, loud and clear:

- **God had sent him**
- **God was truthful**
- **They didn't really know God at all**

That really made them angry!

When people don't understand each other, it's good to sit down and talk things over. But it's more important to listen to one another. And to do that we have to put the other person first. That's the hard part.

You will not find me
John 7:30-36

Jesus said, 'I shall be with you a little while longer, and then I shall go away to him who sent me. You will look for me, but you will not find me, because you cannot go where I will be.' (Verses 33 and 34)

When our children were small, we went to live in Africa for three years. At the airport, my mother and father kissed us goodbye, then watched us go through the gate marked 'Departures only'—their daughter and two precious grandchildren. They loved us, but couldn't go where we were going. They had no passports or tickets. They were heartbroken.

But Jesus was talking to those who hated him, to people who didn't believe that he was God's Son.

He had a very different message for those who loved and trusted him.

Thank you, Lord, that you're our ticket and passport. Amen

The people divided

John 7:37-44

So there was a division in the crowd because of Jesus. (Verse 43)

If the Queen invited you and your friends to Buckingham Palace, would you argue about which bus to catch, until it was too late? Of course not. You'd find out in good time.

The Festival reminded the Jews of all the years they had lived in the desert. It was also a harvest festival. Each day, a priest filled a golden jug with water and poured it over the altar as a thanksgiving. The people waved palm branches and sang hymns. On the last day, they marched round the altar seven times. It was a day they never forgot.

Jesus chose that day to shout his invitation out loud. Whoever believed him would receive the Holy Spirit, like life-giving water, pouring from them and giving life to all. And what did the people do? They argued.

John 7:1-44

Things to do

Chinese whispers

Learn how to listen carefully. Sit in a circle with some friends. One of you choose something to say—for example, 'White mice have pink ears!' Whisper it very quietly into the next ear. Each person passes it on round the circle. The last person says out loud what they think the message is. You'll be amazed how it changes!

Toby + Trish   Shush!

Don't look now, but that man who's just come into church is wearing a lady's hat!

Whoops! It is a lady!

Nobody like him
John 7:45-52

When the guards went back, the chief priests and Pharisees asked them, 'Why did you not bring him?' The guards answered, 'Nobody has ever talked like this man!' (Verses 45 and 46)

Sir Winston Churchill was Britain's leader in World War Two. His radio broadcasts lifted everyone's hopes and spirits. I have a tape recording of some of those speeches—'We shall defend our island, whatever the cost may be... We shall never surrender.' I also have them in a book. I can read them out loud, but it isn't the same at all. Perhaps you can think of other leaders with the same power to inspire people—Nelson Mandela, for instance.

Fiery speeches can be dangerous, as well as encouraging. It's important to listen to the words as well as the voice. God gave Jesus the power to speak in a very special way. But we can listen carefully, and understand his words. And that's what Nicodemus did.

On trial
John 8:1-11

I sneaked some biscuits at teatime and hid them under the bed to eat in the night, only I didn't wake up!

'Whichever one of you has committed no sin may throw the first stone at her.' (Verse 7)

When I was nine years old, I stole a toothbrush. I didn't mean to. I was in the chemist's shop with Mum. She was choosing toothpaste, and I was fiddling around with the brushes. There was a lovely pink one. Mum bought the toothpaste. We were outside the shop. My hand was in my pocket, and the pink toothbrush was in my hand. I was so ashamed and scared. I hid it, then buried it in the garden. I'll never forget that once I was a thief.

Imagine how that woman felt—dragged in front of all the leaders. But Jesus was there. He told her, 'Go, but do not sin again.' And when we admit we've done something wrong, he says the same to us.

Dear Lord Jesus, thank you for forgiving me when I'm sorry for doing wrong. Amen

Jesus the light of the world
John 8:2-20

Jesus spoke to the Pharisees again. 'I am the light of the world,' he said. 'Whoever follows me will have the light of life and will never walk in darkness.' (Verse 12)

My father used to breed chickens at home. He would place the eggs in a special case called an incubator. Then he would switch on a soft, warm light. The chickens grew inside their shells. Then they pecked themselves free and struggled out. The light had given warmth and light. Soon they were running around in the fresh air, under the blue sky.

Here's some simple physics. Neptune, the planet furthest from the sun, is five times colder than Earth. Mercury, the planet nearest the sun, is eight times hotter. Yes, light and warmth and life go naturally together. It's true in physics, and it's true of Jesus, too.

Never alone
John 8:21-30

'And he who sent me is with me; he has not left me alone, because I always do what pleases him.'
(Verse 29)

We never mean to hurt people, especially old friends. It's only when they leave us alone that we begin to wonder—why? Have we forgotten their birthday? Were the batteries flat when we returned that game they lent us? Perhaps we had some good news, and didn't bother to tell them. Whatever it was, we've neglected them—taken them for granted.

Sometimes just a kind word and a smile will put things right. God will always show us a way. There's a golden chain that starts with God and links us, through Jesus, with others. When we're part of that chain, we're never alone.

Dear God, please help me to be a good friend, like you. Amen

The truth will set you free
John 8:31-39

So Jesus said to those who believed in him, 'If you obey my teaching, you are really my disciples; you will know the truth, and the truth will set you free.' (Verses 31 and 32)

Have you ever watched a fly caught in a spider's web? It struggles frantically, but sooner or later the spider will pounce. We feel like that fly when we're trapped in a web of lies. We lie to get out of trouble, but when we're found out, we're in even worse trouble. Telling the truth is the best way of staying free.

But that's not all Jesus meant. If we follow him, we needn't follow the crowd. He teaches us what's right and wrong. We're free to say 'No' to whatever's unhealthy or wrong. We're free to be ourselves, not an imitation or a slave.

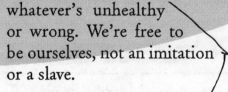

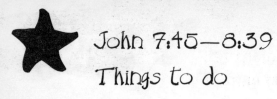

John 7:45—8:39
Things to do

Light and warmth

Jesus, the light of the world, shows us the warmth of God's love. We know how it feels when the sun goes behind a cloud and then finally sets.

How many things can you think of that need light and warmth to grow?

The nearer you get to the sun, the warmer it gets. Right?

So why do you get snow on the top of mountains?

I didn't tell an untruth this morning... Whoops! I've just told another one now!

No joke
John 8:40-47

'When he tells a lie, he is only doing what is natural to him, because he is a liar and the father of all lies.' (Verse 44b)

Some people think the devil is a joke, but Jesus knew better. He'd seen the devil at work for a long time, and he recognized the devil's children.

Jesus had been gentle. He had explained carefully. He had told the truth about his Father God. But these people wouldn't listen. Their arguments were turning nasty. Some of them were plotting to kill Jesus. They declared they were God's children, descended from Abraham. But Jesus told them their father was the devil—a liar and a murderer.

Time was running out. Jesus had to pull out all the stops.

Heavenly Father, I'm so glad that I can trust Jesus, your Son, to tell me the truth. Amen

I've got to ask questions to find out who I am— you just say 'yes' or 'no'

Winnie the Pooh

Jesus and Abraham
John 8:48-59

'I am telling you the truth,' Jesus replied. 'Before Abraham was born, "I Am".' (Verse 58)

Now Jesus was really in trouble. For the Jews, 'I Am' was another name for God. Jesus was telling them plainly, 'I am God.' No wonder there was an uproar.

John tells us that Jesus was with God from the very beginning, before the world was created. He had a human body for only thirty years. But before then, he'd found other ways of meeting people. Abraham, Moses and David had all called him 'Lord' and talked with him. And we can do the same today.

Many people believed Jesus, but his enemies asked, 'Who do you think you are?' As if he hadn't told them! For them, Jesus was not only mad—he was dangerous.

The man born blind
John 9:1–12

'The man called Jesus made some mud, rubbed it on my eyes, and told me to go to Siloam and wash my face. So I went, and as soon as I washed, I could see.' (Verse 11)

I'm making my eyes beautiful by putting cucumber on them

Waste of a good salad!

When I was little, I loved to run and jump—until I tripped over. Then I would howl with pain, blood trickling from a gritty knee. Quick as a flash, Mum would spit on a clean hanky and wipe the dirt away. Soon my knee started to heal.

Healing this man's blindness was easy. The hard part was the question—why was he born blind? People often ask, 'What have I done to deserve this?' But Jesus said that his blindness wasn't a punishment. It was God's chance to show pity and love.

Dear Father, help me to show your pity and love, too. Amen

Don't ask us
John 9:13-23

'Ask him; he is old enough, and he can answer for himself!'
(Verse 21)

A blind man could see, and everyone rejoiced—or did they? Believe it or not, they grumbled. They had two complaints. First, Jesus had cured the man on the Sabbath. So he had broken the law. Second, perhaps the man wasn't really blind. Perhaps someone had been lying, and it was all a trick. They were determined to catch Jesus one way or another.

They started with the man's parents. Those poor people had a real problem. If they were expelled from the synagogue, they would be outcasts. It wasn't like being told they couldn't go to church any more. No, their whole life would be a disaster. No wonder they refused to speak. But there's something more powerful than fear. And that's what Jesus had—love.

The blind man understands
John 9:24-34

'Unless this man came from God, he would not be able to do a thing.' (Verse 33)

Over the centuries, thousands of people have been killed for being Christians. About 1700 years ago, many children were among those who died. They could have saved their lives. All they had to do was to say, 'I don't believe in Jesus.' Because they wouldn't lie, many others believed. Here are some of their names: Basilissa (9), Fausta (13), Eutropia (12), Justus (13) and Pastor (9). They and many others now have 'Saint' in front of their names.

This is the story of another brave man. He could have shrugged and said, like his parents, 'Don't ask me how he did it. He just did.' Instead, he stuck up for Jesus. He said that Jesus came from God. So he was punished. He was made an outcast for telling the truth.

63

John 8:40 — 9:34
Things to do

For the first time

If you want to see something as if for the very first time, look through your legs. You'll see the world upside down. Look at a sunset this way... You'll be amazed!

Toby + Trish — Short back & sides

I feel as though I'm seeing things for the first time!

You are. You've just had a haircut!

Blindness
John 9:35-41

Jesus answered, 'If you were blind, then you would not be guilty; but since you claim that you can see, this means that you are still guilty.' (Verse 41)

If you haven't ever watched a new baby, try now. At first their eyes squint. Then they look towards a light. They begin to see shapes, and their eyes follow movements. After five or six weeks, they see a smiling face, and smile back. Fast work, eh?

But soon they see something they like—and they grab. They have to learn 'No', 'Don't touch', 'Hot!' At last they learn obedience. They learn to 'see' what is right or wrong.

The blind man saw who Jesus was, and he believed. The Pharisees saw, but they didn't believe. So the verdict had to be 'Guilty'.

 Lord Jesus, let my eyes always be open to what is good and true. Amen

I am the gate
John 10:1-10

'I am the gate. Whoever comes in by me will be saved; they will come in and go out and find pasture.' (Verse 9)

It was hard work being a shepherd in Palestine. There wasn't much grass on the rocky hillsides. You had to keep moving, looking for grass, and watching out for wild animals. The shepherd stayed in front, looking out for danger.

When the weather was good, they would stay out all night. The shepherd would lead the sheep into a sheepfold. This had no roof or gate—just a gap in the wall. Once they were inside, he would lie down in the gap. Nothing could get in or out except across his body.

But at sunrise the sheep were free to go out and eat. They had safety and freedom, rest and food. And that's what Jesus offers. I can't think of a better life, can you?

One flock, one shepherd
John 10:11-21

'There are other sheep which belong to me that are not in this sheepfold. I must bring them, too; they will listen to my voice, and they will become one flock with one shepherd.' (Verse 16)

We once had a Siamese cat called Smokey, a bull terrier called Sally and a labrador called Bella. Nobody had told Smokey that he was a cat and that his 'sisters' were dogs. So when they went for a walk, Smokey came too.

Jesus knew that his Father's kingdom wasn't only a Jewish kingdom. He came to be a light for the world. He'd already welcomed Samaritans into his flock. There was just one problem. Jesus wasn't going to be around much longer with a human voice. How were people in Europe, Australia, America and the rest of the world going to hear his voice. Any ideas?

Woof!

Jesus is rejected
John 10:22–31

'My sheep listen to my voice; I know them, and they follow me.' (Verse 27)

Most of the sheep in Palestine were kept for wool, not for meat. So they could live for years. They got to know their shepherd very well, and he knew them. Often he had pet names for them. And when he called, they recognized his voice.

If there was a storm, and two flocks had to shelter in the same cave, the sheep would get mixed up. But the next morning one of the shepherds would go outside and call, and only his flock would run after him.

The people asked Jesus, 'Are you the Messiah?' but when he told them the truth, they tried to stone him. They heard his words, but didn't recognize his voice.

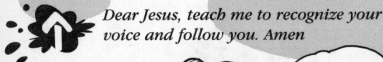

Dear Jesus, teach me to recognize your voice and follow you. Amen

There can't be anyone there, Boomerang... I didn't hear a thing

Just watch him
John 10:32-42

*'Even though you do not
believe me, you should at
least believe my deeds, in
order that you may
know once and for
all that the Father
is in me and that
I am in the
Father.' (Verse 38)*

There's a hilarious chorus in
a Gilbert and Sullivan
musical, *The Pirates of Penzance*. The police are
planning to capture the pirates. But all they do is to
march up and down for ever, singing that they're
going to fight the foe. And someone keeps popping
up to say, 'Yes, but you don't go!'

Jesus didn't just talk about good deeds. He did
them. They proved he was the Son of God. But his
enemies still didn't believe him.

It wasn't all bad news. When Jesus left Jerusalem,
where he was under attack, many believed in him
and followed him.

John 9:35 — 10:42

Things to do

No two sheep are alike

Jesus said, 'I know my sheep and they know me.' Sheep all look alike to us, but there are some differences.

How many differences can you find between these two sheep? There are ten altogether.

Toby + Trish — Sorry, sheep

An urgent message
John 11:1-11

The sisters sent Jesus a message: 'Lord, your dear friend is ill.' (Verse 3)

When my friend was ill, I sent four messages for her:

* To her boss: 'She won't be at work today.'
* To her son: 'Come if you can.'
* To my other friends: 'Please pray for her.'

Yes, that makes three. My first message was to God: 'Please show me how I can help.' And he did. The wonderful thing about Jesus is that he's always ready to help.

When Mary and Martha sent their message, they didn't say, 'Come quickly.' Bethany was very close to Jerusalem, and it may have been dangerous for Jesus to come back so soon. But they knew that Jesus would do whatever was best. They didn't need to tell him what to do.

Dear Lord, thank you that I can trust you to know what I need. Amen

57

Where were you when I needed help with my homework?

Why weren't you there?

John 11:12–22

Martha said to Jesus, 'If you had been here, Lord, my brother would not have died!' (Verse 21)

Martha's words sound like a gentle ticking off, don't they? When something dreadful happens, we want to blame someone. You're in hospital with a broken leg and your friend comes to see you. Instead of being pleased, you tell him, 'If you hadn't thrown the ball so hard, I wouldn't have had to run into the road and...'

After all, it was four days since they'd sent that message. But look what Martha says in the next verse. She doesn't ask Jesus to wave a magic wand. She doesn't ask him to do anything. She just tells him that she knows he is special to God. She trusts him, and that's enough.

By the way, the name Lazarus means 'God is my help'.

Believe in me
John 11:23-31

Jesus said to her, 'I am the resurrection and the life. Those who believe in me will live, even though they die; and all those who live and believe in me will never die.' (Verses 25 and 26)

Gerry was a drug addict and an alcoholic. He was in prison for attempted murder. Now he tells everyone, 'When I met Jesus I became "alive" for the first time in my life!'

There's more than one way of being dead. We say 'My fingers are dead—they can't feel a thing.' 'My hair's lifeless.' 'The telephone's dead.' 'My passport's expired.' We can be alive, but feel useless, good for nothing. Something like greed or selfishness has cut off our lifeline to God.

Jesus promised life to everyone. Whatever we've done in the past, when we believe in him we have a new life, but for ever.

Either it's a very quiet song or my batteries are flat

Jesus in tears
John 11:32-42

Jesus wept.
(Verse 35)

> I feel so sorry for the African children on TV who are hungry

In 1977, Queen Elizabeth visited the island of Fiji. There she unveiled a statue of a great Fijian leader. Someone watched her face as the veil fell from the statue, and heard her say quietly, 'Oh, he's so much like my father.' And there were tears in her eyes. Her father, King George VI, had been dead for many years, but the Queen remembered him with love—and sadness.

It's horrid when you want to cry and someone says, 'Don't.' Tears are natural. They're human. And Jesus was human. He knew that the story of Lazarus would end happily, but his friends were distressed, and he cried with them.

It's good to cheer someone up when they're sad, but sometimes only tears will help.

 Lord Jesus, thank you for being with me when I'm sad. Amen

Lazarus, come out!
John 11:43-48

He came out, his hands and feet wrapped in grave clothes, and with a cloth round his face. 'Untie him,' Jesus told them, 'and let him go.' (Verse 44)

There was no doubt about it. Lazarus was dead. He had been in the tomb for four days. There should have been a bad smell when they took the stone away. Sniff. Very strange. No smell!

If Lazarus had been your friend or brother, you would have peeped into the tomb, wouldn't you? You would have helped him out. But the enemies of Jesus were watching closely. If they'd seen someone go into the tomb, they could have said it was all a trick—that somehow they'd sneaked the living Lazarus into the tomb. But this way there was no mistake. Lazarus had been dead, and now he was alive.

By the way, did you notice that Jesus prayed before he called Lazarus out?

John 11:1-48

Things to do

Hot off the press

The headlines in a newspaper always give the hottest news. Make a front page about Lazarus with a 'hot off the press' headline.

Toby + Trish   Tomorrow's news

There's nothing good in this newspaper

There will be tomorrow—fish and chips!

Ready...
John 11:49–57

From that day on the Jewish authorities made plans to kill Jesus. (Verse 53)

I wish John had told us what Jesus said to his disciples during those days in the desert. We can only guess.

Jesus knew his time was nearly up. He had to get ready for what was coming. So he left Bethany, and went into the desert again. Back in Jerusalem, his enemies were also plotting. They feared that Jesus could destroy the whole nation. He had to be eliminated.

When we know there's trouble ahead, we can do what Jesus did. We can take time to be quiet, if only for a few minutes. We can talk to a friend, or read a favourite Bible verse. We can tune in to God, offload, and take his peace on board.

Do not disturb for five minutes

Dear God, thank you for reminding me that I can spend time with you, as Jesus did. Amen

Thanks, Boomerang, is that for me? Oh, I see, you want me to throw it!

Steady...
John 12:1-8

'You will always have poor people with you, but you will not always have me.' (Verse 8)

Wendy was only six when she came to stay with us. She was painfully shy. She hardly ever spoke, and only in whispers. When she and her mother were leaving, Wendy held out her hand. On it was a pretty brooch. I thought it might be a present for her granny, so I said, 'That's lovely.' I didn't touch it. She looked so hurt. 'Don't you want it?' It was for me—a present chosen with great care. It was the only way Wendy knew of saying 'thank you'.

For many of us, saying 'thank you' is easy. But for others, like Mary, it's very hard. Only something chosen with care and given with love could show how she felt.

Go!
John 12:9-16

So they took branches of palm trees and went out to meet him, shouting, 'Praise God! God bless him who comes in the name of the Lord! God bless the King of Israel!' (Verse 13)

From the desert, back to Bethany, and now—Jerusalem. Things were hotting up. The chief priests had heard all about Lazarus being brought back to life, so they decided to kill him as well.

It only took half an hour to walk from Bethany to Jerusalem. Jesus had often done it. But this time he ordered a donkey to ride on. The disciples didn't understand. But the crowds knew the signs. If a king rode into a city on horseback, it meant war. If he rode on a donkey, he brought peace. Now many believed in Jesus—and called him King. First Lazarus and now this—no wonder the chief priests were alarmed.

Great glory!
John 12:17-26

'I am telling you the truth: a grain of wheat remains no more than a single grain unless it is dropped into the ground and dies. If it does die, then it produces many grains.' (Verse 24)

I found a packet of sunflower seeds in the garden shed. They had been hidden for years. What a waste! Think of all the sunflowers I could have grown—and hundreds more from their seeds.

Jesus knew he must give his life for others. This was to be his glory. And he wants us to do the same. He wants us to give up our selfish life. Like a sunflower seed, if I bury it, something beautiful will grow in its place.

By the way, did you notice who introduced those Greeks to Jesus?

Lord Jesus, I want to bury the selfish 'me' and grow something good instead. Amen

Jesus is troubled
John 12:27-36

'When I am lifted up from the earth, I will draw everyone to me.' (Verse 32)

'Lifted up' meant crucifixion—a slow, painful death. Only thieves and murderers were executed that way. Jesus had to become the lowest of the low, the scum of the earth.

No wonder the people were puzzled. If Jesus was the Messiah, why should he die so horribly? They knew that the Messiah would live for ever. Even when God spoke to them, they still didn't understand. No wonder Jesus went away alone once more.

Whatever Jesus did, he did properly. To be a real man, he must be born, he must live, and he must die. But Jesus always thought first of his Father, and others. He wanted glory for his Father, and life for us with him.

⭐ John 11:49—12:36

Things to do

Top donkey

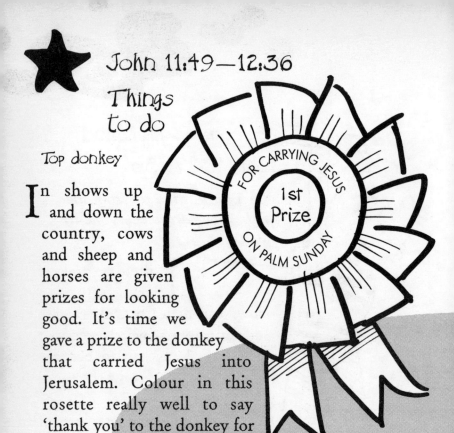

In shows up and down the country, cows and sheep and horses are given prizes for looking good. It's time we gave a prize to the donkey that carried Jesus into Jerusalem. Colour in this rosette really well to say 'thank you' to the donkey for doing a good job. (First prizes are always red.)

FOR CARRYING JESUS
1st Prize
ON PALM SUNDAY

Toby + Trish Top donkey

I wonder if the donkey that Jesus rode on was related to the one that carried Mary to Bethlehem?

Open eyes and closed minds
John 12:37-43

Even though he had performed all these miracles in their presence, they did not believe him. (Verse 37)

Joe's family arrived at the airport. They had their tickets and passports. Their luggage was checked in. Then they sat and waited.

Over the loudspeaker they heard, 'Passengers for Flight 22, please go to Gate 11.' Joe's dad said, 'Plenty of time. I'll find something to read.' Then there was a second announcement: 'Flight 22 is now boarding at Gate 11.' Joe's mum said, 'Plenty of time. I'll get some extra toothpaste.' There was a third announcement: 'Passengers for Flight 22, please hurry. Gate 11 is about to close.' Joe said, 'Wait a minute, my shoelace is undone.'

When they got to Gate 11, it was closed. They'd missed the flight.

Dear Jesus, please help me to hear you, and believe. Amen

Saving life
John 12:44-50

'If anyone hears my message and does not obey it, I will not judge him. I came, not to judge the world, but to save it.' (Verse 47)

Next time you have fire drill at your school, watch your teacher. When the alarm sounds, you line up quietly and go to your space in the playground. Then comes the important part—your teacher opens the register, and calls out your names. It's vital to make sure everyone is out of danger. There may be one person who wasn't in the room. Perhaps they'd been fooling around in the cloakroom. That's not important. Whatever they've done, they mustn't be left in the burning school.

That's how Jesus feels. He can't force you to follow him to safety. But he's willing to go back into that burning building to look for you.

The hour has come
John 13:1–11

Jesus poured some water into a basin and began to wash the disciples' feet and dry them with the towel round his waist. (Verse 5)

Have you flown in an aeroplane? The journey to the airport seems to take for ever. At the airport, your luggage is weighed and tickets and passports checked. Then you hang around and wait. Even when you're on board, everything has to be checked carefully. You begin to think you'll never get off the ground. But at last the engine roars, and you're racing down the runway.

For Jesus, it was almost lift-off time. But there was still time to teach his disciples a few things, like:

- How to help others.
- How to let others help you.
- Even when you've had a bath, you still need to wash the dust of the day's journey off your feet.
- How to love someone who doesn't love you.

Always learning
John 13:12-20

'I, your Lord and Teacher, have just washed your feet. You, then, should wash one another's feet.' (Verse 14)

Growing up is like an obstacle race, and the first hurdle is to learn to do things for yourself. It's a great feeling when you button your coat for the first time. Everyone's so proud of you.

The next big leap is when you can help somebody else. You fetch Grandad the newspaper, or help to lay the table. You feel so grown-up. But the novelty wears off. We become selfish. We don't want to waste our precious time on other people. Jesus knows that this is the greatest obstacle to growing up—learning to put others first.

Lord Jesus, thank you for coming to help. Please show me how I can help others, the way you showed your disciples. Amen

Betrayed
John 13:21-30

After Jesus had said this, he was deeply troubled and declared openly, 'I am telling you the truth: one of you is going to betray me.' (Verse 21)

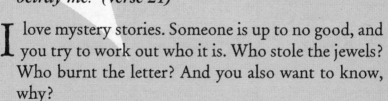

I love mystery stories. Someone is up to no good, and you try to work out who it is. Who stole the jewels? Who burnt the letter? And you also want to know, why?

But in this story, Jesus knew the answers. Judas was a thief. The other disciples had loving hearts, but Judas was greedy and jealous. There was no room in his heart for love.

Even so, there was still time for Judas to change. Jesus gave him one last chance. The bread dipped in sauce was a sign of love. As long as there was a chance of his love getting through to Judas, Jesus kept trying. No wonder he was troubled.

John 12:37—13:30
Things to do

Obstacle race

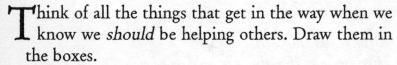

Think of all the things that get in the way when we know we *should* be helping others. Draw them in the boxes.

Watching...	Lying on...	Lying in...
Kicking...	Playing with...	Eating...

Toby + Trish — **Obstacle race**

Rubbish! I could jump through that

You're smelly, you're a nuisance and you're always hungry. But I love you!

A new commandment
John 13:31-38

'And now I give you a new commandment: love one another. As I have loved you, so you must love one another.' (Verse 34)

I say 'I love you' to my family. I even say it to my goldfish. It's easy, because I know that they love me. (Well, the goldfish wag their tails at feeding time.)

But Jesus said, '...as I have loved you'. And how had he loved them? He'd spent time with them. He'd been patient when they hadn't understood. He'd forgiven them when they'd been selfish. He'd loved Peter even when he knew Peter would deny knowing him. He'd loved Judas even when he knew Judas would betray him.

Love isn't just a warm, cosy feeling. It can be painful. It can be costly. But nobody forces us to love. We can choose to love people we don't even like!

A place for you
John 14:1-11

'Do not be worried and upset,' Jesus told them. 'Believe in God and believe also in me. There are many rooms in my Father's house, and I am going to prepare a place for you.' (Verses 1 and 2)

Jenny and Ben were going to a holiday camp for the first time. Ben didn't like the idea. 'What if my bunk's too high, and where will I put all my things?' But he needn't have worried. They had a chalet near the swimming-pool, with lots of space, and a bunk-bed just the right height. Ben sighed, 'It's heaven!'

The brilliant thing about heaven is that Jesus knows exactly what's right for each of us. It's not like a holiday camp, where we might be lucky or we might not. Our best friend says he'll make a place specially for us, so just relax—and stop worrying.

Reserved

I just thought I'd jot down a few things I want to pray for!

Never alone
John 14:12-2Ø

'If you ask me for anything in my name, I will do it.' (Verse 14)

There's a Hebrew prayer, 'God save us from praying travellers.' Sounds strange, doesn't it? Until you remember that everyone who travels on Monday prays, 'Please don't let it rain today', and everyone who travels on Tuesday prays, 'Please don't let it rain today', and so on. So if God answered everyone, the world would die by Sunday!

God doesn't need 'shopping list' prayers. He already knows what we need, including things we haven't even dreamed of. That's why we need to pray in his name. When we pray on our own, we often get it wrong. But God sent a Helper, the Holy Spirit, to pray with us and for us.

Thank you, God, for sending the Holy Spirit to help me when I pray. Amen

Small word, big meaning
John 14:21-31

'Peace is what I leave with you; it is my own peace that I give you. I do not give it as the world does. Do not be worried and upset; do not be afraid.' (Verse 27)

Sometimes parents sigh, 'Peace at last' when the children go to bed. We often pray for peace in troubled lands. But peace doesn't only mean the end of fighting. The Hebrew word 'Shalom' means peace. But it also means good health, sound sleep, safety, contentment and friendship. It's used as a lovely daily greeting.

Jesus wants us to leave all our worries and fears with him. When we do, we have the 'Shalom' that his Father promised. When King David was surrounded by enemies, he could still say, 'When I lie down, I go to sleep in peace; you alone, O Lord, keep me perfectly safe.'

Remain in my love
John 15:1-10

'I am the real vine, and my Father is the gardener.' (Verse 1)

L ong ago, in Old Testament times, Israel was called God's grapevine. He brought the people of Israel out of Egypt, and planted them in a new land. But the people disobeyed God. Their enemies attacked, and the vineyards were ruined. In Psalm 80 the people pray, 'Come and save this grapevine that you planted, this young vine.'

Jesus called himself the real vine, but his branches, the people, were still disobedient. When a grapevine gets out of hand, it sends out wild shoots. It wastes its strength and gives a poor crop. So God, the gardener, has some serious pruning to do. He loves the vine too much to let it go to waste.

 *Dear Lord, help me to grow and be fruitful. Amen*

John 13:31—15:10

Things to do

Branches everywhere

Lots of our High Street shops have branches everywhere. So does Jesus—you and me!

As one of Jesus' branches, see how much 'fruit' you can grow. Every time you do something for Jesus—like smiling when you don't feel like it, or doing something for someone you don't like— colour one of the grapes in the picture with a purple crayon. No cheating, now!

Toby + Trish — Improved Fruit

Think what Jesus could have done with the rest of his life if he hadn't given it up for me!

Amazing love
John 15:11-17

'The greatest love a person can have for his friends is to give his life for them.' (Verse 13)

Jesus is amazing. He gave his life to make our lives real. But people can be amazing, too. Ordinary people have given their lives for others. During World War Two, Corrie ten Boom's family hid Jewish friends from the Nazis, in their home in Holland. Some of the family paid with their lives. Corrie's sister was with her in a concentration camp, and died there. But Corrie was able to forgive her enemies.

Even in your town there may be people who've rescued others from burning buildings or flooded rivers. Yes, Jesus is amazing, and with his love and courage people can be amazing, too.

 *Dear Jesus, thank you that people still give their lives for others, as you gave yours for me. Amen*

Toby always sticks up for me (except when I stay off school)

An ugly word
John 15:18-25

'Whoever hates me hates my Father also.' (Verse 23)

Corrie ten Boom had to watch her sister, Betsy, being persecuted by the Nazis. For her, it was worse than being ill-treated herself. It's horrible when people say nasty things about someone we love. We have to stick up for them, don't we? We feel like hitting out at the ones who've said those things. So we can understand how Jesus felt. He was also saying that he and God are one.

But Jesus isn't thinking only about himself. He's thinking about all those who belong to him. And if we follow Jesus, that means us. Those who hate him will hate us, too. We have to decide for ourselves: do we want to belong to Jesus? Is he worth sticking up for?

In touch
John 15:26—16:7

'The Helper will come—the Spirit, who reveals the truth about God and who comes from the Father. I will send him to you from the Father, and he will speak about me.' (Verse 26)

We have family and friends all over the world—and a telephone. When we heard of a disaster in Sri Lanka, we phoned our friends there and asked, 'Are you all right?' Yes, they were, and they were so pleased that we'd worried about them. We can tell them our good news, too.

In Jesus' time there were no telephones, no faxes or e-mail. Jesus could only speak to a few thousand people. And time was running out. But God has something better than e-mail for us—the Holy Spirit. If we believe in Jesus, the Holy Spirit, the helper, keeps us on line.

Hiya, Brian! Could you do the arithmetic homework?

79

Wait a while
John 16:8-15

'I have much more to tell you, but now it would be too much for you to bear.'
(Verse 12)

I'll tell you more when I see you tomorrow

After the car crash, I wrote to my parents, 'We're in hospital. We've had an accident, but we're both OK.' They were on the other side of the world, and they didn't know I'd been unconscious for four days! Later I told them about the wrecked car and broken bones. All that mattered at first was that we were alive!

Jesus says that the Spirit will lead us into all the truth. The truth won't be zapped to us all at once. Sometimes we say, 'Slow down' when we're puzzled. Or, 'I can't bear it' when news is bad. But some stories are too good to rush. We want to savour them slowly, a page at a time. Nobody knows all this better than Jesus.

Sadness and gladness
John 16:16-24

> Guess what, Boomerang! Dinner time at last!

'Now you are sad, but I will see you again, and your hearts will be filled with gladness, the kind of gladness that no one can take away from you.' (Verse 22)

When we took our children to Africa, their grandparents were heartbroken. But the following year they came to visit us. They had a brilliant time. They saw hippos, crocodiles, elephants, lions—and their grandchildren. The happy times made up for the sad goodbyes.

If all this is true of human families, who never get things absolutely right, just think how it will be when Jesus' friends meet him again. Our time of family fun didn't last for ever, but Jesus promises the kind of gladness that no one can take away. Wow!

Heavenly Father, when we're sad, help us to remember your promise of gladness to come. Amen

99

John 15:11—16:24
Things to do

Welcome home

Someone you love is coming home and you are going to have a party. Think what you will need in order to celebrate. Use your ideas to finish the picture.

Be brave!
John 16:25-33

'The world will make you suffer. But be brave! I have defeated the world!' (Verse 33b)

Peter Pan is one of my favourite stories. I've read the book and heard it on radio. I've seen it on stage and at the cinema. Each time, I've understood something I hadn't understood before. It's the same with many good stories.

It was hard for the disciples to understand everything Jesus had to tell them. He's tried telling them in different ways. Three times he said, 'I have told you this so that...' And now he tries again, this time more plainly than ever. Some of it is hard to take. They will have to share his suffering. But they'll also share his victory. He tells them plainly that God loves them. And that's worth being brave for.

I think I ought to pray for my friends. I'd like a few more of them, please!

Jesus prays for his disciples
John 17:1-8

'And eternal life means knowing you, the only true God, and knowing Jesus Christ, whom you sent.' (Verse 3)

Imagine it. You know what's coming—betrayal and a cruel, painful death. So what do you do? You pray. And what do you pray? Help! Of course you do. Even people who don't believe in God pray when things get tough—when the house is on fire, or when someone they love is ill.

Yes, but this isn't you or me. It's Jesus. See what Jesus prayed. (It's the longest prayer in the Bible.) He prayed a long, loving prayer for his friends. But first he talked to his Father. He talked about giving glory to the Father, and eternal life to his friends. God first, then his friends, himself last of all.

Dear Jesus, you prayed for your friends first. Help me to do the same. Amen

Keep them safe
John 17:9-19

'I do not ask you to take them out of the world, but I do ask you to keep them safe from the Evil One.' (Verse 15)

Every time I saw Matt, he had a leg or arm in plaster. His mother was in despair. 'How can I stop him climbing trees?' she wailed. Well, she could keep him in bed all day long but, knowing Matt, something would still go wrong.

Jesus knows there are worse things than catching measles or falling out of a tree. The Evil One is another name for the devil, and Jesus has already called him a murderer and a liar. In fact, he's the opposite of God, who gives life and truth.

> I had been warned about going too fast on my bike, so I went slowly and fell off!

Because the devil is a liar, he can make bad things look good. That's why it's important to stay close to God—and the truth.

Not only for them
John 17:20-26

'I pray not only for them, but also for those who believe in me because of their message.' (Verse 20)

Jesus loves me— pass it on...

Jesus loves you— pass it on

Now we're beginning to see how the story goes. Jesus tells the disciples about his Father's kingdom. They tell other people. Word gets around. And it ends up with us, two thousand years later.

Yes, this is the amazing part—Jesus is praying for you and me! We're the ones who've received the message. Jesus wants every one of us to be with his disciples, with him, and with his Father, to see his glory, and share his love. Sometimes it's hard to believe we're really lovable. Whenever you feel that way, just read these verses again.

Dear Lord Jesus, thank you for praying for me all those years ago. And thank you that the disciples obeyed you. Amen

Betrayal
John 18:1-11

Simon Peter, who had a sword, drew it and struck the High Priest's slave, cutting off his right ear. The name of the slave was Malchus. (Verse 10)

Imagine the scene—bright lanterns and torches (even though it was moonlight). Soldiers and armed guards, and Peter with a sword. And all this for one man! No wonder Peter did something crazy.

But Jesus stayed calm. He told them quietly that he was the one they were looking for. When he spoke, some fell to the ground. Was that because he said, 'I am...'? Did they believe he was God? We can't be sure. He asked them to let his disciples go. He could have escaped, but he knew what he must do. And here's some good news, which John doesn't tell us, but Luke does: Jesus heals poor Malchus' ear!

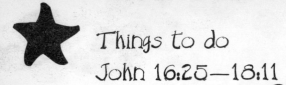

Things to do
John 16:25—18:11

Shadow theatre

Cut one side off an empty cereal packet and cut a square hole in the other side. Using sticky tape, attach a white cloth over the square hole. Copy the trees and the soldier in the picture on to thin

Copy this tree twice

Make five soldiers on one strip

White cloth

Trees

Fold

Fold

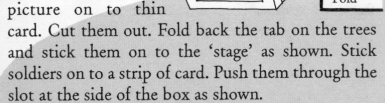

card. Cut them out. Fold back the tab on the trees and stick them on to the 'stage' as shown. Stick soldiers on to a strip of card. Push them through the slot at the side of the box as shown.

Darken the room and shine a torch behind your theatre. This is how it would have looked when the soldiers came to arrest Jesus in the garden.

Toby + Trish — Lost shadow

Peter Pan lost his shadow and Wendy sewed it on again for him

If you believe that, you'll believe anything. I wouldn't sew anything on for you!

Peter denies Jesus
John 18:12-18

The girl at the gate said to Peter, 'Aren't you also one of the disciples of that man?' 'No, I am not,' answered Peter. (Verse 17)

Poor Peter. He has chopped someone's ear off. And now Jesus is tied up and led away by soldiers and guards. Not long before, Peter had told Jesus, 'I am ready to die for you.' But now he doesn't know what to do—except to try to keep warm, and wait. He stays as close as he dares. He's recognized. He denies knowing Jesus.

Peter's a strange mixture, like many of us—trying to be brave, getting some things right, some things wrong. But the important thing about Peter is that when others ran away, he didn't.

Thank you, God, that however scared we get, we never need to run away from you. Amen

> With Boomerang by my side I'd never run away... or would I?

No secrets with Jesus
John 18:19-27

'I have never said anything in secret. Why, then, do you question me? Question the people who heard me. Ask them what I told them—they know what I said.' (Verses 20b and 21)

Jesus was right. At a proper trial they would have asked witnesses, not Jesus. But this wasn't a proper trial. It was late at night. All they wanted was to get rid of him—quickly.

But we're not on trial. We're free to examine the evidence. We can read what Jesus said. We can discover what he did. He kept no secrets from us. If something puzzles us, we can ask questions. We don't have to sneak around in the dark. That's freedom!

Peter was still around. Then it happened: he denied Jesus for the third time. Imagine how he felt when that cock crowed.

Pilate questions Jesus
John 18:28-36

Jesus said, 'My kingdom does not belong to this world; if my kingdom belonged to this world, my followers would fight to keep me from being handed over to the Jewish authorities. No, my kingdom does not belong here!' (Verse 36)

I once called a little girl 'Princess Jane'. She laughed and said, 'I'm not a princess.' So I asked her, 'Isn't God your Father? And isn't he a king?' Jane thought for a minute. Then she agreed that he is, so she must be a princess after all!

Pilate was the Roman governor. His job was to collect taxes for the emperor and keep everything peaceful. If Jesus wanted to be king in place of the emperor, he needed to know. So Pilate asked Jesus, and Jesus told him the amazing truth—his kingdom was already here!

Jesus deserved to be crowned— but not like that!

What is truth?
John 18:37—19:5

So Jesus came out, wearing the crown of thorns and the purple robe. Pilate said to them, 'Look! Here is the man!' (Verse 5)

Ross came home from school looking miserable. His mother asked, 'Has someone been bullying you?' He burst into tears. 'It's worse than that—they laughed at me.'

Yes, there are worse things than being beaten up. The Roman soldiers bullied Jesus. They had sliced his skin open with a whip. Long, sharp thorns had torn his scalp. There was blood everywhere. Then they jeered and mocked him. Pilate could have set him free, but the people chose a bandit instead.

Pilate looked for the truth, and found an innocent man. People don't always like the truth. If we try to tell them the truth about Jesus, some may laugh at us. If that happens to you, remember that it happened to Jesus first.

There are lots of crowds on TV getting angry and burning flags

Crucify him!
John 19:6-16

Then Pilate handed Jesus over to them to be crucified. (Verse 16)

We were in Peru when there was a big demonstration— an anti-British demonstration! Thousands of people marched through the streets, shouting slogans and waving banners. My family hid in a shop. I don't suppose the crowds would have hurt us, but we were scared.

The crowds in Jerusalem were getting ugly. Pilate tried talking to Jesus. He tried talking to the leaders of the crowd. But it was no use. They hated Jesus. They wanted him dead.

It's exciting to be in a crowd, waving and cheering. There's a great feeling of power. But we must always remember what Jesus told Pilate: the only real power is from God.

Dear God, when we're in a crowd, please help us to remember that you are the only real power. Amen

111

John 18:12—19:16

Things to do

The dark side of the moon

The trial of Jesus broke all the rules. The Sanhedrin was not supposed to meet at night or force witnesses to speak. Why did they do it? To get Jesus condemned under cover of darkness.

ARRESTED AT NIGHT

Here's a picture of the full moon that was shining down that night. Use a saucer or a CD as a template to cut out a circle of card. On one side write, 'The light of the world' and colour it in bright colours. On the other side write, 'Arrested at night' and colour it in dark colours.

LIGHT OF THE WORLD

Toby + Trish   Forgotten moon

It's funny how everybody notices an eclipse of the sun, but nobody bothers about the moon

Jesus is crucified
John 19:17-22

Pilate wrote a notice and had it put on the cross. 'Jesus of Nazareth, the King of the Jews' is what he wrote. (Verse 19)

Before the notice was put on the cross, it was paraded through the streets of Jerusalem. Jesus followed, carrying the heavy wooden cross on his bleeding back. That way, everyone knew who was going to be crucified, and why.

Pilate hadn't wanted Jesus to die. He'd only done what the crowds wanted. But he wouldn't change that notice. They asked him, but he refused. Pilate had asked Jesus, 'What is truth?' And there it was, printed in three languages on the notice! Yes, Jesus is the King of the Jews, but he's also King of heaven and earth!

If someone had to write a notice telling the truth about you, what would you like them to write?

This should not be happening to Jesus

Life and death
John 19:23-27

Jesus saw his mother and the disciple he loved standing there; so he said to his mother, 'He is your son.' Then he said to the disciple, 'She is your mother.' (Verses 26 and 27)

My brother was ill in bed, and children were laughing and playing outside in the street. I wanted to rush out and stop them, but I didn't. They didn't know he was dying.

For the soldiers, this was just another job. As usual they threw a dice to decide who got the prisoner's clothes. He wasn't going to need them any more.

Jesus was in agony. But he still thought of his mother and his best friend. And he didn't just say, 'Look after my mum.' He held an adoption ceremony in front of witnesses: 'She is your mother. He is your son.'

Dear Jesus, thank you for loving us so much, even on the cross. Amen

I've done it!
John 19:28-30

Jesus drank the wine and said, 'It is finished!'
Then he bowed his head and died. (Verse 30)

Matthew, Mark and Luke tell us something that John doesn't tell us: Jesus gave a loud cry. Yes, this was a shout of triumph. Jesus had crossed the finishing line. He'd scored the winning goal. He'd put the last piece of the puzzle in place. He'd done everything his Father had sent him to do.

John gives us two signs to help us understand. He reminds us of Psalm 69: 'When I was thirsty they offered me vinegar.' (Vinegar was like sour wine.) He reminds us of the night the Israelites escaped from Egypt, by marking their doors with hyssop dipped in blood. (Hyssop is a herb with many uses.) Jesus had completed something that started way back in history. The wine and hyssop were two important clues.

Two precious signs
John 19:31-37

One of the soldiers, however, plunged his spear into Jesus' side, and at once blood and water poured out. (Verse 34)

When prisoners had hung on the cross for a long time, the soldiers broke their legs. That made their bodies drop, so that they choked. It speeded things up. The soldiers could see that Jesus was dead. But just to make sure, one of them speared him through the heart. He hadn't been dead very long. Blood ran from the heart, and water from around the heart.

For John, these were two more important signs. First, Jesus had said, 'My blood is the real drink.' It was a sign of sacrifice. And Jesus had said, 'Whoever drinks the water that I will give him will never be thirsty again.' He was the water of life. Blood and water—two more pieces of evidence.

First at the cross
John 19:38-42

What's that you're reading?

Nicodemus, who at first had gone to see Jesus at night, went with Joseph, taking with him about 30 kilogrammes of spices, a mixture of myrrh and aloes. (Verse 39)

It's the Bible. It's great!

In some parts of the world, it's dangerous to be a Christian. People are killed just for reading the Bible. They are thrown into jail for meeting to worship Jesus.

Nicodemus and Joseph had been secret disciples. They were members of the Council which had condemned Jesus! They had both protested, in vain. A few days before Jesus died, he said, 'When I am lifted up from the earth, I will draw everyone to me.' Well, it was happening already. Nicodemus and Joseph couldn't keep away. They were being very brave. Their secret was out.

Dear Lord Jesus, help me to be brave like these two men, and not to be your disciple only in secret. Amen

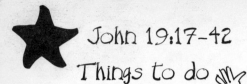

John 19:17-42

Things to do

Three leaps for joy!

In a famous book called *Pilgrim's Progress*, the hero of the story, Christian, carries a heavy burden on his back. When he comes to the foot of Jesus' cross, the burden rolls off and he gives three leaps for joy. It is amazing that one of the saddest events in the history of the world can make us so happy. Christian's story is a picture of why this is so—Jesus died for us!

Colour in the picture of Christian, or draw one of yourself leaping for joy.

Toby + Trish — High jump

Toby would be a great high jumper if he found he'd come top in the exams every day!

18

What's going on?
John 20:1–10

She went running to Simon Peter and the other disciple, whom Jesus loved, and told them, 'They have taken the Lord from the tomb, and we don't know where they have put him!' (Verse 2)

Three people in a hurry, rushing around and confused. John—some say he was the disciple Jesus loved—ran and saw for himself. Then Simon Peter pushed past him and barged in. But Mary had got there first. And when the others had gone home, Mary stayed.

The authorities had tried to make sure the body didn't disappear. If it did, the disciples could say that Jesus had been resurrected, proving that he'd told the truth! Matthew tells us that they sealed the tomb and put a guard on it. And what did these three find? The tomb was open, and the body had gone. No wonder they were confused!

Mary knew Jesus was alive because he spoke to her—and he speaks to me, too

Mary sees Jesus
John 20:11-18

Jesus said to her, 'Mary!' She turned towards him and said in Hebrew, 'Rabboni!' (This means 'Teacher'.) (Verse 16)

When something mind-blowing happens, it takes time to sink in. We say, 'I don't believe it!' or 'It's not true!'

Simon Peter and John had told Mary what they had seen, and she was too upset to take it in. But God doesn't leave us upset for long. Because he loves us, he helps us to sort things out. First he sent his messengers—angels—to tell Mary the good news. Then Jesus himself spoke to her. That's the kind of friend he is. If he can't get through to us one way, he tries another. He wants to be sure that we know he's alive.

Dear Father God, when we're confused, please give us the patience to wait for a message from you. Amen

Filled with joy
John 20:19-23

It was late that Sunday evening, and the disciples were gathered together behind locked doors, because they were afraid of the Jewish authorities. Then Jesus came and stood among them. 'Peace be with you,' he said. (Verse 19)

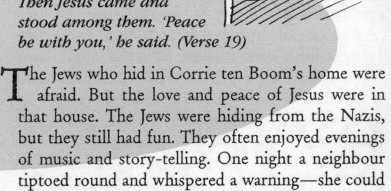

The Jews who hid in Corrie ten Boom's home were afraid. But the love and peace of Jesus were in that house. The Jews were hiding from the Nazis, but they still had fun. They often enjoyed evenings of music and story-telling. One night a neighbour tiptoed round and whispered a warning—she could hear them singing!

Locked doors might keep the enemy out, but they can't keep Jesus out. He filled his disciples with joy and peace. He asked them to carry on the work God had given him. But first he gave them the Holy Spirit. He never asks us to go it alone.

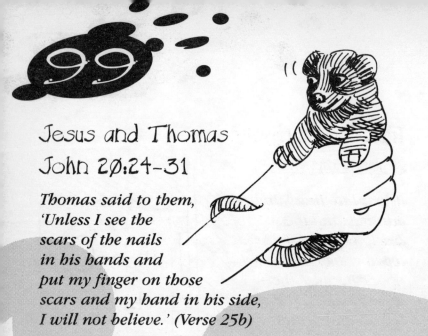

Jesus and Thomas
John 20:24-31

Thomas said to them,
'Unless I see the
scars of the nails
in his hands and
put my finger on those
scars and my hand in his side,
I will not believe.' (Verse 25b)

Janet lived in a wild part of Uganda, where she used to take care of orphaned animals. One day, a man brought her a small creature from the jungle. Janet was amazed: 'It's a potto!' When an expert heard about this, he said, 'Rubbish! There are no pottos in Uganda.' Then he went to see for himself. He apologized to Janet. It was a potto!

We can't see Jesus with our own eyes, but we can see him in other people—in their joy and peace; in their lives. We can believe—and be happy.

Dear Lord, we're glad you show
yourself in many ways, so that we
can really know you. Amen

Try something simple
John 21:1-8

He said to them, 'Throw your net out on the right side of the boat, and you will catch some.' So they threw the net out and could not pull it back in, because they had caught so many fish. (Verse 6)

They were nearly home. It had been a long night, and they were tired. Someone was standing on the shore. They didn't recognize him, but for some reason they did what he said. First, he was polite and friendly. In the Good News Bible, Jesus calls them 'young men'. Other Bibles say 'friends'. He wasn't asking anything difficult—just one last try. And he wasn't making fantastic promises—just 'You'll catch some.'

A familiar voice, a friendly word, a simple idea that worked like crazy—it all added up. No wonder they recognized him.

Dear Lord, when you ask me to try something, I'll trust you. Amen

John 20:1–21:8

Things to do

Joy in the garden

Make an Easter garden. Line the top half of a cardboard egg box with foil and fill it with earth or sand. Cut out one of the egg holders from the bottom of the box and set it on its side in the corner of the garden to make the empty tomb. Use moss, small stones and tiny plants to create your garden. Or you could cut up an old sponge and paint it green to make bushes.

Cover the tomb with moss or green tissue paper to blend in with the rest of the garden. Find a larger stone and place it rolled away from the entrance of the tomb. Make a tiny stone path leading up to the tomb and place some tiny strips of white material or tissue paper inside to show that Jesus has risen from the dead.

Toby + Trish Garden joy

You just think everything is dead in the garden after winter

Then new life starts coming up everywhere

A lakeside barbecue
John 21:9-14

Jesus said to them, 'Come and eat.' None of the disciples dared ask him, 'Who are you?' because they knew it was the Lord. (Verse 12)

There are all kinds of barbecues. Some are bring-your-own-sausages. Others are posh, expensive affairs. But this must be the most amazing barbecue of all time. A glowing fire on the beach; fish sizzling; eight old friends, and one of them Jesus. Jesus was doing what he'd always done—teaching, guiding, serving, and giving. And it was a bring-and-share barbecue. The disciples had something to give, too.

> The last supper was sad, but the last breakfast was happy!

They were scared to ask, but they already knew who he was. They had seen him handing out bread and fish once before. Jesus probably spoke the same blessing this time as he'd done then.

Once we get to know Jesus, we don't need to keep asking, 'Who are you?'

I have to say everything at least three times to Boomerang—except 'Dinner'!

Three times
John 21:15-19

A third time Jesus said, 'Simon son of John, do you love me?' (Verse 17a)

Breakfast was over. The sun was rising. All those fishes had to be sorted out. But Jesus spent a few precious moments with Simon Peter—just the two of them.

They had some unfinished business to clear up, the business of Simon Peter saying he wasn't a disciple—three times. Now Jesus got Simon Peter to say 'I love you'—three times. Three chances to make up for what he'd done. And three chances to hear what Jesus wanted him to do. Jesus had said, 'I am the good shepherd', and now he asks Simon Peter to carry on that work. What an honour!

Dear Jesus, you give us the chance to put things right, and then give us something special to do for you. Thank you. Amen

John's work ended
John 21:20-25

Now, there are many other things that Jesus did. If they were all written down one by one, I suppose that the whole world could not hold the books that would be written. (Verse 25)

Some people keep a diary. 'Got up. Had my breakfast. Cleaned my teeth.' John didn't need a diary. He had a good memory, and a burning love for Jesus, the Son of God.

John spent seventy years remembering, listening to others, gathering clues, hearing the evidence, and writing it down. He's told us that Jesus is the Light, the Word, the Way, the Truth, the Life, the Water, the Bread, the Good Shepherd, and many other things. The never-ending story of Jesus is the greatest ever told—and now we're part of it. Isn't that amazing?

See you in the next Amazing Book!

Dear Father God, thank you that John wrote down the story of Jesus. Please help me to tell it to others. Amen

Look out for Toby & Trish and...

The Amazing Book of Mark by Peggy Hewitt

Meet Jesus—the most amazing person who ever lived! Mark's stories are so real that we feel we're there actually watching Jesus, the man of action who had such a powerful effect on Mark's own life.
£3.99   ISBN 1 84101 049 9

The Amazing Book of Jonah by Peggy Hewitt

Meet hot-headed Jonah—who is famous for doing the wrong thing for the wrong reason! But if Jonah hadn't had such a whale of a time we might never have had the chance to hear why the message that God had for him was so amazing.
£3.99   ISBN 1 84101 055 3

The Amazing Book of Acts by Margaret Withers

Read about Peter and Paul's amazing adventures—written by Luke, who actually saw what happened. Because he wrote everything down, we too can join in the adventure!
£3.99   ISBN 1 84101 100 2

Available from your local Christian bookshop or, in case of difficulty, direct from BRF.

Tel: 01865 748227;
Fax: 01865 773150;
E-mail: enquiries@brf.org.uk